AT THE SERVICE OF DESTINY

AT THE SERVICE OF DESTINY

A Biography of the Living
Moroccan Sufi Master
Shaykh Mohamed Faouzi al-Karkari
may God sanctify his secret

By the disciple **Jamil Zaghdoudi**

Translated from the French
by **Edin Lohja**
and edited
by Dr. **Yousef Casewit**

LES 7 LECTURES

At the Service of Destiny is published by the nonprofit organization *Anwar* and his publishing house *Les 7 Lectures*

44, Fernand Brunfaut Street
1080 Brussels, Belgium

ISBN: 978-2-930978-40-6
Deposit number: D/2019/14.291/13
Legal Deposit: October 2019

بسم الله الرحمن الرحيم
والصلاة والسلام على أشرف المرسلين
وعلى آله وأصحابه أجمعين

Contents

Introduction 13
His Name and his Family 17
His Initiatic Chain of Transmission 19
His Lineage 23
His Birth 31
His Childhood and Youth 35
At the Service of Destiny 39
The Fire of Repentance 49
"Verily, I have Forgiven You" 61
Rapture and Wayfaring 67
Divine Permission *(idhn)* 85
The Shaykh 89
His Character 99
His Knowledge 107
His Physical Appearance 111
His Worship and Exertion 113
His Saintly Miracles 117
Conclusion 133

"God will send to this Nation at the beginning of every one hundred years a renewer *(mujaddin)* who will revive for it its religion."

The Prophet Muḥammad ﷺ

Introduction

In the Name of God
the Compassionate, the Merciful

May the peace and blessings be upon our Messenger and Prophet ﷺ, the master of the two worlds, the isthmus of the two seas, the seal of existence, and the hidden ocean, our Master Muḥammad ﷺ. And greetings upon his Companions and his Household.

Through this book I wanted to convey my understanding of the story of our Shaykh, Sīdī Mohamed Faouzi al-Karkarī, may God sanctify his secret. Besides the honor of receiving most of the information contained herein directly from the lips of our Shaykh, I have also gathered some information from his closest disciples. Thus, I must thank Sīdī Abdel-Nasser,

Sīdī ʿAbd al-Ḥafīẓ, Sīdī b. Siniy, and Sīdī Muḥammad Fadhil for their help and their accounts.

A disciple who succeeds upon the Path is one who is extinguished in the presence of his spiritual master. And only the one who becomes the latter's shadow can be extinguished in him. To this effect, our Shaykh, Sīdī Mohamed Faouzi al-Karkarī – may God sanctify his secret – says in one of his poems,

Is it myself or my shadow that you see?
This can be grasped only by him who has become like me.

The sincere seeker is the one who strives to emulate his Shaykh in all of his actions. To achieve this, he must know and follow his Path. This is the reason why I undertook the writing of this book; to enable its readers to taste from far and nigh the spiritual states of the People of God. This work consists of brief and concise chapters that are arranged chronologically. I implore God to forgive our shortcomings and to guide us upon the Translucent Path *(al-maḥajja al-bayḍā')* whose night differs not from its day, a Path of Light and of divine knowledge, a Path of upright conduct and hope.

You should know, dear reader, that the state of this noble Shaykh is unique and without parallel. We wish, by the grace of God, to share with you what we have heard during our three years of withdrawal from the workaday world in the Karkariyya *zāwiya.*[1] This then is the actual biography of this Shaykh, the spiritual trainer, Sīdī Mohamed Faouzi al-Karkarī – may God sanctify his secret –.

1 *Zāwiya* is a Sufi lodge. Al-Aroui is a small town of approximately 50,000 people in the Nador Province of northeast Morocco.

His Name and his Family

He is the sun of knowledge, the meeting of the two seas, the ocean of gnosis, the inmost heart of the spirit, the red sulphur, the inheritor of the secret of the essence, and the guide upon the Path of unveiling. He is the spiritual trainer, Shaykh Abū ʿAbd Allāh, Sīdī Mohamed Faouzi b. Ṭayyib al-Karkarī – may God sanctify his secret – of noble Prophetic descent, through Idrīsī and Ḥasanī lineage.

Sayyidī Shaykh (lit. my lord, the master) Mohamed Faouzi al-Karkarī married the noblewoman of *Sharīfan* lineage, the pious and chaste *lalla* Najet, may God reward her for her sacrifices for the Path. From this union six children were born, namely: Wihem, Abdullah, Aya, Ala, Wala', and Hira. These offspring go to show the goodness and sacrifices of our master's wife towards the followers of the Path. Throughout the years she worked tirelessly to feed the disciples who stay at the *zāwiya*. In return God bestowed her with a penetrating eye and several unveilings which, in most cases, proved to be true. Thus, we have heard Sayyidī Shaykh Mohamed Faouzi al-Karkarī say: "God has given me the right to have three more wives, but she has earned my pleasure through her sacrifice, selflessness, and character, and therefore I shall not marry any other woman."

Our Shaykh's sanctity is also visible in his progeny, and each of his children bear a prophetic mark. When this mark is inspected closely, one sees that it consists of a birthmark in the form of a map which covers with an astonishing precision all the lands that were tread by the Prophet ﷺ during his life. The most remarkable feature is not the repetition of the mark in each of his children, but the fact that before the birth of his fourth daughter, Wala', he told us: "The next one will be born a few days from now, and you will see, she will have the same mark on such and such a spot of her body." And indeed this is what transpired. This prophetic mark proves the nobility of their lineage.

His Initiatic Chain of Transmission

His chain of transmission goes back uninterruptedly to the Messenger of God ﷺ in the following manner:

Shaykh Sīdī Mohamed Faouzi al-Karkarī al-Ḥasanī al-Idrīsī.

Shaykh Mūlāy al-Ḥasan al-Karkarī.

Shaykh Mūlāy Ṭāhir al-Karkarī.

Shaykh Aḥmad b. Muṣṭafā al-ʿAlāwī al-Mustaghānimī.

Shaykh Muḥammad b. al-Ḥabīb al-Būzīdī.

Shaykh Muḥammad b. ʿAbd al-Qādir al-Wakīlī, known as Shaykh b. Qaddūr al-Wakīlī.

Shaykh Abī Yaʿzā al-Mahājī.

Shaykh Mūlāy al-ʿArbī b. Aḥmad al-Darqāwī.

Shaykh ʿAlī b. ʿAbd al-Raḥmān al-ʿUmrānī, known as al-Jamal.

Shaykh al-ʿArbī b. Aḥmād b. ʿAbd Allāh al-Fāsī.

Shaykh Aḥmad al-Fāsī.

Shaykh Qāsim al-Khaṣṣāṣī.

Shaykh Muḥammad b. ʿAbd Allāh b. Maʿan al-Andalusī al-Fāsī.

Shaykh ʿAbd al-Raḥmān b. Muḥammad al-Fāsī.

Shaykh Yūsuf b. Muḥammad al-Fāsī.

Shaykh ʿAbd al-Raḥmān al-Majdhūb.

Shaykh ʿAlī al-Ṣanhājī.

Shaykh Ibrāhīm al-Faḥḥām al-Zurhūnī.

Shaykh Aḥmad b. Aḥmad al-Burnūsī al-Fāsī, known as Zarrūq.

Shaykh Aḥmad b. ʿUqba al-Ḥaḍramī.

Shaykh Yaḥyā b. Aḥmad al-Qādirī.

Shaykh ʿAlī b. Muḥammad b. Wafā.

Shaykh Muḥammad b. Wafā.

Shaykh Abī Sulaymān Dāwud b. ʿUmar al-Bākhilī.

Shaykh b. ʿAṭāʾ Allāh al-Iskandarī.

Shaykh Abū al-ʿAbbās al-Mursī.

Shaykh Abū al-Ḥasan al-Shādhilī.

Shaykh Abū ʿAbd Allāh ʿAbd al-Salām b. Mashīsh al-Ḥasanī al-Idrīsī.

Shaykh Abū Zayd ʿAbd al-Raḥmān al-Ḥasanī al-ʿAṭṭār, known as al-Ziyyāt.

Shaykh Taqī al-Dīn.

Shaykh Fakhr al-Dīn.

Shaykh Nūr al-Dīn.

Shaykh Muḥammad Tāj al-Dīn.

Shaykh Muḥammad Shams al-Dīn.

Shaykh Zayn al-Dīn al-Qazwīnī.

Shaykh Abī Isḥāq Ibrāhīm al-Baṣrī.

Shaykh Abī al-Qāsim Aḥmad al-Marwānī.

Shaykh Abī Muḥammad Saʿīd.

Shaykh Saʿd.

Shaykh Fatḥ al-Suʿūd.

Shaykh Saʿīd al-Ghazwānī.

Shaykh Abī Muḥammad Jābir b. ʿAbd Allāh.

The pure and purified *Sayyidunā* al-Ḥasan b. ʿAlī.

The gate of the city of knowledge *Sayyidunā* ʿAlī b. Abī Ṭālib.

The master of the two worlds, the Light of the universe, the Prophet and Messenger of God, the beloved, *Sayyidunā* Muḥammad ﷺ.

His Lineage

He is the son of the noble *Sharīf*, Sīdī Mūlāy Ṭayyib al-Karkarī al-Idrīsī al-Ḥasanī, son of the teacher, the Shaykh, the Pole of his time, and the inheritor of the initiatic secret, Sīdī Mūlāy al-Ṭāhir al-Karkarī, may God sanctify his secret, son of Mūlāy Muḥammad al-Fardiy, son of Mūlāy Ṭayyib, son of the Shaykh and Pole Sīdī Muḥammad b. Qaddūr al-Bukīlī, son of Mūlāy ʿAbd al-Qādir, son of Mūlāy Aḥmad, son of Mūlāy al-ʿArbī, son of Mūlāy Muḥammad, son of Mūlāy ʿAlī, son of Mūlāy Mūsā, son of Mūlāy ʿAlī, son of Mūlāy Yaʿqūb, son of Mūlāy Ibrāhīm, son of Mūlāy b. Zayd, son of Mūlāy Yaḥyā, son of Mūlāy ʿAbd al-Raḥmān, son of Mūlāy ʿAbd Allāh, son of Mūlāy ʿAbd al-ʿAzīz, son of Mūlāy Zakariyyā, son of Mūlāy Yaḥyā, son of Mūlāy al-Ḥasan, son of Mūlāy

Muḥammad, son of Mūlāy ʿAlī, son of Mūlāy ʿĪsā, son of Mūlāy Maymūn Abū Wakīlī, son of Mūlāy Masʿūd, son of Mūlāy ʿĪsā, son of Mūlāy Mūsā, son of Mūlāy ʿAzzūz, son of Mūlāy ʿAbd al-ʿAzīz, son of Mūlāy Maʿzūz, son of Mūlāy ʿAllāl, son of Mūlāy Jābir, son of Mūlāy ʿImrān, son of Mūlāy Sālim, son Mūlāy ʿIyyāḍ, son of Mūlāy Aḥmad, son of Mūlāy Muḥammad, son Mūlāy al-Qāsim, son of Mūlāy Idrīs al-Azhar, son of Mūlāy Idrīs al-Nafs al-Zakiyya, son of Mūlāy ʿAbd Allāh al-Kāmil, son of Mūlāy Ḥasan al-Thānī, son of Mūlāy Ḥasan al-Sibṭ, son of *Sayyidunā* ʿAlī – may God ennoble his face – and of Fāṭima al-Zahrāʾ, daughter of the Master of the two worlds, *Sayyidunā* Muḥammad.

On his mother's side, he is the son of *lalla* Yamna who was the paternal cousin of *Mūlay* Ṭayyib, and the grand-daughter of Mūlāy Muḥammad al-Fardiy, and a niece of Mūlāy Ṭāhir, may God sanctify his secret. A shrine with a dome has been erected for each of his ancestors in the precincts of the town of al-Aroui. Many of them, besides being scholars of the Law, were granted the direct knowledge of God, which made them realized knowers through God. Thus, I have heard Sayyidī Shaykh Mohamed Faouzi al-Karkarī say, "This blessing *(barakah)* has been transmitted from father to son over many generations."

His family has settled for twelve generations in the town of al-Aroui, located in the Rīf region of northern Morocco, twenty kilometers from the city of Nador.

Among the members of his family we can mention Sīdī Mukhtar Bukhnif who was known for his numerous saintly miracles *(karāma)*, such as the folding of space in order to offer the Friday prayers at the holy city of Mecca. A Moroccan traveler who had just performed the pilgrimage lost his money and found himself unable to return home. As he was lamenting his situation some Meccans advised him to go find a certain Moroccan who was not known by anybody and who always offered his Friday prayers at a precise spot in the mosque.

Following their advice, the traveler found Sīdī Mukhtār Bukhnif at the indicated place. After he explained his situation, he was told by Sīdī Mukhtār to return the following week, as he would find a solution to his problem. When they met the following week, Sīdī Mukhtār asked the traveler to keep his eyes closed until he told him to open them. He did so, and when he opened his eyes after a few moments he found himself in his village and could see his family. This traveler became Sīdī Mukhtār's closest devotee, and when the latter passed away, he ordered all the way from Fes a hand-carved dome made of a very heavy, precious wood, which required great efforts to be brought from a distant city, at a time when cars and modern means of transportation did not exist.

Sīdī Abū al-Mawāhib b. Qaddūr al-Bukīlī – may Allah sanctify his secret – a paternal and maternal ancestor of Sayyidī Shaykh Mohamed Faouzi al-Karkarī as well as a member of the initiatic chain of the fifth generation was a great master of the Path. He was the first to settle in Mount Karkar which is located some forty kilometers outside of al-Aroui, hence the surname Karkarī. His disciple was Sīdī Muḥammad b. al-Habib al-Bouzidi who spread the teachings of the Path through his heir, Sīdī Aḥmad al-ʿAlāwī, as well as through Shaykh Muḥammad al-Hibrī, founder of the Hibriyya Path whose branches extended throughout the Maghreb in the wake of the Belqaydiyya in Algeria. He transmitted the mysteries of the Supreme Name Allāh and the initiatic sciences so well, that he was named "the man of divine bestowals" (Abū al-Mawāhib).

Sīdī Muḥammad al-Fardiy – may God be pleased with him – great-grandfather of Sīdī Mohamed Faouzi al-Karkarī was known for his piety and sincerity in both words and deeds. It has been related that Mūlāy al-Ṭayyib – may God have mercy on him – emphasized sincerity and honesty in the education of his son, Sīdī Muḥammad al-Fardiy.

One day he decided to send his son to Fes, during the colonial period, and it so happened that the group with which he traveled reached a checkpoint that the invaders had set up to search the passengers. They never stopped anyone with money or any object of value on them without confiscating it. So they questioned all the travelers on the bus one by one, and naturally, everybody said they had no money with them. They started searching everyone until they reached Sīdī Muḥammad al-Fardiy whom they asked, "Do you have any money with you?" He said, "Yes." "How much?" they asked. "I have this much…", he answered. Everybody started making fun of him, "You have that much money?!" The officers finally let him go [without confiscating his goods], and this is how his honesty enabled him to escape that day. Indeed, God granted him with numerous astonishing saintly miracles.

Sīdī Muḥammad al-Fardiy is buried at the *zāwiya* of Sīdī b. Qaddūr al-Būkīlī on Mount Karkar. A number of mausoleums and domes were erected over his tomb to honor his sanctity, but each time they collapsed. A local *Sharīf* saw Sīdī Muḥammad al-Fardiy in a dream, telling him: "I want no domes over my tomb, it is disrespectful towards my father." Today, instead of a dome grows a tree with its branches stretching over his grave and providing a grand entrance to the *zāwiya*.

Sīdī Mūlāy Ṭāhir al-Karkarī – may God sanctify his secret – the paternal grandfather of our Shaykh — may God make us benefit from them — went to find the master of his age, Shaykh Aḥmad al-'Alāwī – may God sanctify his secret – in *zāwiya* of Mostaghanem in Algeria. In Shaykh 'Adda Bentounes' (d. 1952) biography of the life of Shaykh al-'Alāwī entitled "The Splendid Garden: on the Traces of al-'Alawī," *(al-Rawḍa al-Saniyya fī al-ma'āthir al-'Alawiyya)*, it is reported that Mūlāy Ṭāhir was accompanied by

Sīdī Muḥammad al-Ṣaghīr, and that Shaykh Aḥmad al-ʿAlāwī got up and went to meet them in person.

Likewise, the book mentions that Mūlāy Ṭāhir was granted the station of guidance *(irshād)* during the lifetime of his Shaykh: "One of these *zāwiyas* is that of the noble Shaykh, Sīdī Mūlāy Ṭāhir b. Muḥammad b. Qaddūr al-Karkarī, which is located in the city of Temsaman. As for his arrival at Mostaghanem we already mentioned Sīdī Muḥammad al-Ṣaghīr b. Sīdī Mūlāy al-Ṭayyib, and we said that both of them were authorized by al-Ustadh (Sīdī Aḥmad al-ʿAlāwī) to give the litany *(wird)* of the order *(ṭarīqa)*, and Shaykh Sīdī Mūlāy Ṭāhir received his authorization to take charge of the training of dervishes *(fuqarāʾ)* as well as transmit the spiritual lore of the order through the invocation *(tadhkīr)*. And indeed, God enabled him to transmit the grace to them in the best manner, by training people whom God had predestined to be the protectors of this noble Path as well as of his rightly guided children."[2]

2 Shaykh Adda Bentounes, *al-Rawḍa al-saniyya*.

Sīdī Mūlāy Ṭāhir – may God sanctify his secret – fought alongside the pious warriors *(mujāhidīn)* during the resistance against the Spanish colonizers in the Moroccan Rīf. There was a cave under his *zāwiya* in the village of Temsaman in northeast Morocco that served as a refuge and warehouse for the fighters. After the war, the cave became a place of retreat for seekers in which numerous disciples had spiritual openings *(fatḥ)*. Mūlāy Ṭāhir married seven women with whom he had forty-three children, most of whose descendants live in Temsaman. Among his children is the father of our Shaykh, Sīdī Mūlāy Ṭayyib, may God shower blessing upon blessing on him.

His Birth

Sīdī Mūlāy Ṭayyib, son of Mūlāy Ṭāhir and father of Sayyidī Shaykh Mohamed Faouzi al-Karkarī – may God sanctify his secret – dedicated himself fully to the service of his father even though he was not initiated at his hands. His selfless dedication and love for his father made him his favorite son. Always by his side, Mūlāy Ṭayyib drove his father to all his meetings and visits. In his youth he went to Europe to work. This distance saddened Mūlāy Ṭāhir profoundly. When his son returned for a visit, in order to prevent him from leaving once again, Mūlāy Ṭāhir married him to the daughter of his brother, the pious and modest *lalla* Yamna, may God cover her with His mercy. Moreover, Mūlāy Ṭāhir offered him the room in which he lived, an outhouse of the Temsaman *zāwiya* in the

Moroccan Rif, a region whose people are known for their faith and courage.

From this union, Sayyidī Shaykh Mohamed Faouzi al-Karkarī was born on Wednesday July 2, 1974 (12 Jumada al-Thani 1394 AH) that same room. His surname was chosen by Mūlāy Ṭāhir himself.

Nowadays, most of the *zāwiya* where have started to fall apart except for the room were our Shaykh was born. By the grace of God we were able to visit it several times. The *zāwiya*, made of stone and mud, is located at the summit of a hill, surrounded by fields of crops, facing the Mediterranean Sea. On top of the hill Mūlāy Ṭāhir's tomb is now covered by a conic dome, while Mūlāy Ḥasan's tomb is at the opposite lower corner. Facing the *zāwiya* is a small mosque that was built at the hill of the hill and it is here where Sayyidī Shaykh and Mūlāy Abdel-Nasser would memorize the Qur'ān as children. Despite this area being strictly Berber, all of Mūlāy Ṭāhir's children and grandchildren speak exclusively in Arabic, which is a trait of the noble *Sharīfian* families. After his father's passing, Mūlāy Ṭayyib built a mausoleum with a dome above it with his own hands, and it can still be seen today.

Among the many signs of our Shaykh's sanctity — for those gifted with a perceptive heart — is the fact that all his brothers and sisters possess birth certificates with both *Hijri* and Gregorian calendar dates, except Sayyidī Shaykh whose date of birth is registered only in the solar calendar.

His Childhood and Youth

He grew up under the aegis of his parents and his grandfather, witnessing the religious rites within the Temsaman *zāwiya*. Mūlāy Ṭāhir who was known for his strict and uncompromising nature went as far as flogging his disciples and children when they deviated from prophetic orders, and despite having forty three children and dozens of grandchildren, he was particularly gentle with the young Mohamed Faouzi, so much so that many of his family members became jealous. When asked why he held the then two year old Mohamed Faouzi on his lap from morning to evening, Mūlāy Ṭāhir would respond: "If you find a child like this bring him to me, but you shall find none." He knew through unveiling what his grandson would become.

While still a child Sayyidī Shaykh Mohamed Faouzi al-Karkarī – may God sanctify his secret – was distinguished from other children by his seriousness, rather than idleness, distraction, and sloth. Thus, our Shaykh's brother, Sīdī Abdel-Nasser, says, "While still a child, he was hardly inclined towards playing. His exceptional nature could be seen at a young age. His clothes were never stained or ripped, but were always tidy. He would not run around, as all children do, but was always calm."

From an early age, he also had veridical visions that were actualized in the corporeal realm *(mulk)* just as he had witnessed them in the spiritual realm *(malakūt)*. I once heard him say, "As a child I had several visions during sleep, and after some time they were actualized in the sensorial world. I became aware of this after having visited, during a vision, a fully packed house. After some time I went with my parents to visit one of my aunts. Upon entering her place, I recognized the house that I had seen in my vision. I was even able to tell with precision which piece of furniture was located behind this or that door. When I realized this, the dreams continued to reveal themselves to me. However, I quickly noticed that if I shared my dream with someone they would cease occurring. Thereafter, whenever I would see that something bad was about to happen, I hastened to relate my dream."

Mūlāy Ṭayyib married a second wife who settled in the town of al-Hoceima, in the Moroccan Rif. It is in this city that, surrounded by his father and step-mother, Sayyidī Shaykh Mohamed Faouzi al-Karkarī began his elementary studies. He was later sent to a boarding school in the town of Taza of the region of Fes to complete his secondary education. He explains that "Morocco's boarding schools do not resemble those in Europe, but nevertheless this was the best education."[3]

[In his teenage years,] God in His infinite wisdom willed that Sayyidī Shaykh interrupt his studies in order to begin his apprenticeship of the world, until he carried the banner of sanctity.

3 He said during a conversation with the *fuqarā'*: "For those who wish to live in the *zāwiya*, there is no better example for them than military service or boarding schools. If I could, I would send all my disciples to the army in order to learn order and discipline before they come to the *zāwiya*."

At the Service of Destiny

In his teens, Sayyidī Shaykh Mohamed Faouzi al-Karkarī started working in a fish factory to help his family. In addition to this labor, he sold fish and clothes in the marketplace. During this time, he experienced great inequities and went through numerous trials, and his relationship with his stepmother became so complicated that the world seemed too narrow for him, death being preferable to life.

In reference to this trying time, I once heard him say,[4] "Even I, your Shaykh, committed a sin greater than all your sins put together before meeting my Shaykh. In our family, prayer, invocation, and abstinence were common things, praise be to God for all

4 On April 30, 2018.

His graces, but there came a time when the world became too narrow for me, and one day I sent my brother Abdullah to buy some juice and about one hundred poisonous pills for me... A single pill of those could kill three dogs.

"I bought one hundred pills that day. My parents had brought us up religiously, and recalling some ḥadīths as I was taking the pills I knew perfectly well that my place would be in Hell. I knew that, as the ḥadīth puts it, I would be condemned to perform my action perpetually in Hell... I knew it. I also recall that when I took the poison the call for the afternoon prayer was announced. I went to the mosque, with poison in my stomach, and prayed the two cycles in reverence for the mosque.

While praying, I swear, I have yet to pray like that day... In every prostration it was as if I would not get up again, and while standing up I would see the Name Allāh in front of me on a decoration. I was waiting for death and the hellfire. I prayed to God to not cut my prayers off with my death, and indeed I was able to complete them. As I was leaving the mosque I fell to the ground."

Sayyidī Shaykh Mohamed Faouzi spent those three days, from Wednesday to Friday, unconscious and beside himself, between life and death. God sent him a vision in that state, which he related to us as such: "I saw myself in a type of tribunal. There were several men in front of me, who seemed like judges. I saw them discuss my case among themselves until one of them turned towards me holding his hammer, and slamming it forcefully he said, 'Mohamed Faouzi al-Karkarī is condemned to ten years in prison.'"

He woke up from his coma by the call for Friday prayers, which he attended. There was no trace of poison left in him; it was as though he had never taken the pills. A few days later, aged nineteen, his spiritual state became so intense that he was isolated from his family and friends, and undertook a trip across Morocco. He visited several cities, reached distant places on foot, and walked among mountains and valleys. He said, "My family thought that after my suicide attempt I would start again. For them I was virtually dead."

Our Shaykh's brother, Sīdī Abdel-Nasser told us: "I still remember the day. He was with the dervish *(faqīr)* Ibn al-Siniy. After receiving a telephone call, he left... It was the last time that I saw him for the next ten years."

The young Mohamed Faouzi then went to Nador accompanied by *Sharīf* b. al-Siniy,[5] and spent what was left of his money for the ticket to the farthest destination he could afford; the city of Taza, where his boarding school was located. Then he continued his trip to Fes.

I heard him say about this experience: "The first night that we spent outside was on a road leading to the city of Sefrou,[6] and the first city in which we stayed was Fes, close to the gate of Boujloud (bāb bujlūd), a few meters from the taxi station... We did not know anyone, but after some time I recognized the different quarters of Fes, Mont-Fleuri, Zouagha... I remember a mosque where we spent many nights. After Fes, we travelled on foot all the way to Oujda where we stayed for three months. Then we went

5 Sīdī Muḥammad b. Siniy Taibi told me: "I accompanied him until Nador, he only had sixty six dirhams with him. He lent me fifty and kept the remaining sixteen, and then he left. From that day I had no news of him for ten years."

6 In Berber, "the city of the hideout."

to Nador for three days, and finally to al-Hoceima where we spent a week. After al-Hoceima we walked all the way to Oued Laou.[7] We would sleep under trees, and whenever hunger seized us, we ate leaves. Following Oued Laou, we continued our trip towards Tétouan, then Tanger, and we returned to Fes again. From Fes we headed for Marrakech where we only spent two days, and we continued our trip towards Chichaouga, Agadir, Ouarzazate, Tiznit, Tafraout, Houara,[8] until we reached Mahbes,[9] during the first year of the militarization. We went back to Agadir and continued on to Rabat, in the suburb of Temara, where we stayed for quite a while, followed by Kenitra. I am only mentioning the cities, and not the towns and villages, such as Qacem, Marmousha, al-Hajeb, Ifran, Ain Rahma, Mūlāy Ya'qub, 'ayn Shadya...

A year had passed since our initial departure. The second year, we started the Dour, visiting one *moussem*[10] after another for forty-four saints buried within

7 In the Tétouan region.

8 Ouled Teima.

9 He adds, "I saw from afar a heap of clay indicating the border."

10 Religious festival, often held in honor of a saint.

Moroccan territories. We slept in shrines and tombs of saints, such as Sīdī Mūlāy 'Abdullāh Amghār, where we stopped for a good while. We visited the *moussem* of Shaykh al-Kamel, the commemoration *(moussem)* of Sīdī 'Alī b. Ḥamdūsh, Sīdī Idrīs al-Azhar, and Mūlāy Idrīs al-Akbar. Sometimes we would make thirty rounds between two tombs. In some cities, we spent a whole year, in others seven months, and in others only a few days. Hence, when a disciple tells us today that he comes from such and such city, we know who he is, because we have learned the characteristics of the inhabitants of that city during our pious roaming *(siyāḥa)*, whether they are stingy or generous, gentle or rough..."

Shaykh Mohamed Faouzi al-Karkarī – may God sanctify his secret – sometimes spent days and entire months alone crossing fields and mountains, sleeping wherever night time would seize him. "I took the earth as my bed, and the starry sky as my blanket. I travelled across the mountains but I entrusted my luggage with God… I was serving destiny without knowing it. Whenever I would supplicate God, He would respond to my supplication. Whatever I sought

I obtained. Wherever I went, God's creatures turned towards me," he says.

While the days of hunger went on, our Shaykh would eat from garbage containers. In that state, he would hear trees and rocks speak to him and converse with him. He recalls, "We had isolated ourselves from people, and this made us talk to trees and rocks. We cannot keep count of all the saintly miracles that we experienced during those years of wandering."

He continues, "We lived with people whom you cannot imagine. We lived with the most degraded and humiliated people that exist, and yet we saw ourselves as more degraded than them because we believed that whatever they did would never equal the evil we had committed. We tried to take our lives, and God says that whoever slays a soul...it is as though he slew all of mankind.[11] This is the reason why when someone comes to us now, no matter what his past is, he leaves us having turned to God in repentance. You may well preach to him *(daʿwah)* all your life, but you will never affect him. Why? Because you

11 Qur'ān, 5:32.

have not experienced these states. You cannot guide or instruct someone if you have not walked the same road. Among those whom you call sinners, evil men, drunkards, and prostitutes we have encountered the most elevated men and women *(ʿillīyīn)*, and we witnessed a hidden mercy in them. In some cases, these people become the best. When we became a Shaykh those whom we considered the most elevated proved to be the vilest *(suflī)*, and this only added astonishment to our astonishment."

Among the trials that our Shaykh had to endure during those years of wandering was that in one of the jobs that he found he was accused by a fellow employee of stealing. The police came to interrogate him, and just as they were about to imprison him a man recognized him and witnessed in his favor by saying, "Among all the people on earth, he is the only one who could never steal, leave him alone." It was later revealed that he was the person who had accused our master of theft while being guilty of it himself, and he was imprisoned for this.

Thus did he travel unaware of God's plan. God wanted him to keep company with all of His creatures, be they pious or sinners, and that he partake in their states and their lives, until he became the teacher of states. He kept company with vagabonds,[12] drunkards, drug addicts, without ever being affected by their sins. In spite of the hardship of the weather and the traveling, he never neglected prayers, which he always offered in their due times. How can one guide a fornicator without knowing his problems? How can one guide the rascal or the drug addict without ever bothering to visit them, as if our life can be reduced to a theoretical science? Thus did God perfect his training of the soul, making him a mercy unto men, be they pious or sinful.[13]

He told us once, "During my ten years of wandering I would often wonder, 'O God, why did I have to go through all of this? What have I done to deserve

12 He says, "I stayed almost three years with a friend, no one knew me better than him."

13 Once when he was travelling across Morocco, he joined a group of vagadonds in the city of Taza, who lived under trees. A young pregnant woman came to ask for their help because she had conceived before marriage and had to flee her family until she would give birth to her infant. All the vagabonds as well as the young Mohamed Faouzi took care of her. Each one of them would bring a daily provision to help her meet her needs until she gave birth.

this?' But only after I met my master was I able to understand." Ten years had passed since his departure, during which his family and friends had no news of him. Then came the time for his return. Recalling his return he says, "Those ten years felt like twenty, because time on the streets passes slowly. When I returned everything had changed, my brother who was a child when I left had become a man, our house was completed, some family members had married, and others had become parents." During his travels, he had become accustomed to placing his complete trust in God. He had abandoned all help coming from anyone else until he succeeded in finding repose only in Him. Then came the time for his intimate union *(wiṣāl).*

The Fire of Repentance

Although our Shaykh's master, Mūlāy al-Ḥasan, was an accomplished master of the Path, he was not known by everyone. His sanctity was so concealed that even his own family did not know his spiritual stature. To this effect, Sīdī Abdel-Nasser, our Shaykh's brother, said: "When I was young I told my mother, may God embrace her in His mercy, that I was going to travel to Egypt to visit Shaykh Kishk[14] to seek the blessings flowing from his hands. She responded by saying, 'You need not go all the way to Egypt for that. Go to your own uncle instead, he is a Shaykh and has inherited from your grandfather.' Back then, while still a child, I did not know that I was going to visit him daily.

14 Shaykh ʿAbd al-Ḥamīd Kishk (d. 1996) was a popular Egyptian scholar and preacher.

Mūlāy al-Ḥasan was known for his good humor and his smiling countenance. They all describe him as gentle, smiling, and generous. Thus, Sīdī *Ḥājj* Muḥammad Fadhil[15] told me: "I have known Sayyidī Shaykh Mohamed Faouzi al-Karkarī since he was a child. His father, Mūlāy Ṭayyib, had a dental office just next to my electrician shop. During his weekly trips to Nador, Mūlāy Ḥasan – may God be pleased with him – usually paid a visit to his brother, Sīdī Mūlāy Ṭayyib. Upon seeing me, he would spread his arms and hug me.

Mūlāy Ḥasan possessed an undeniable beauty *(jamāl)*, and would always smile. I never saw the slightest trace of irritation in him. His stature was strong, and he always wore white. Likewise, he possessed great generosity. Whenever he invited people to his place, he welcomed them in the best manner, and never ate from what he served. He also ate very little. He would often say to his brother, 'So and so should join us in Temsaman', but alas, I was young and did not understand."

15 He was one of the first disciples in the Path.

Sayyidī Shaykh Mohamed Faouzi al-Karkarī – may God sanctify his secret – said concerning Mūlāy al-Ḥasan, "He was sheer beauty *(jamāl)*, and even in moments when he could become irritated, his face reflected joy and good humor so clearly that one could not help but laugh."

Sīdī Abdel-Nasser al-Karkarī said: "He was sheer beauty… he was known for his great generosity, and he invited people daily. Both pious persons and sinners could be found at his place, as he never discriminated between them. All were equal to him. He would never leave without distributing all he had to the needy and the children."

Some time after his return our Shaykh went with his father to visit his uncle, Mūlāy al-Ḥasan, for the occasion of the Eid al-Fiṭr, the feast of fast-breaking at the end of the month of Ramaḍān.

Concerning that occasion, Sayyidī Shaykh Mohamed Faouzi says, "Before joining the Path, I participated in an evening in the presence of the person who would become my spiritual master, Mūlāy al-Ḥasan – may God have mercy on him. We spent that evening at his place with our father and he started discussing with some of his family members on the divine attributes of God and His beautiful names. Having been touched to the depth of my soul by his discussion I started recalling the sins I had committed, and this is how the fire of repentance seized me. At the end of the evening, once everybody had left, I went to meet Mūlāy al-Ḥasan and asked him, 'O uncle, I want to repent. Does God accept my repentance?' Noticing my state, Mūlāy al-Ḥasan began to weep and said to me, 'If you wish to repent, it is because God has already pardoned you.' I then asked him to initiate me and transmit to me the litany *(wird)*, and he said, 'When I return from Rabat I will give you the litany and will initiate you, but in the meantime go back home.' I therefore returned home with my father, and while he and a family member were discussing in the car I could not stop thinking about turning to God in repentance.

When we reached our home, everyone went to their rooms. I could not sleep that night. Having been raised in the *zāwiya* of Mūlāy Ṭāhir, I knew that a novice had to invoke the divine name Allāh, and I did just this until the dawn prayers, after which I fell asleep. When I got up, I went to my father's room and continued my invocation. It was as if the world became too narrow for me [once again]. I went out to offer the voluntary morning prayers *(ḍuḥā)* at the mosque and then returned in the presence of my father, but that state kept increasing to the extent that I felt I was going to implode from within.

I told my father, 'Grant me permission to go to Mūlāy al-Ḥasan.' My father replied, 'We just returned from him and you want to go back already! What for?' I told him, 'Father, I want to make a spiritual retreat *(khalwa)*!' That was indeed my intention. I thought that one could enter into the spiritual retreat whenever one wished. When he heard this, his eyes filled with tears, and he told me, 'Let me give you some change for the taxi'. But I had one hundred *dirhams* which my aunt had given me – may God have mercy on her. When he finally gave me permission to go to Mūlāy al-Ḥasan it was as if the gates of heaven opened for me. I remember going down the stairs of our house in all speed, and seeing my mother prepare the meal. She asked me to sit at the table but I refused, despite her insistence. As I was going downstairs, I asked myself, 'What is this beard on my face? Perhaps I was not sincere in growing it... Hence, I went to the barber and asked him to shave both my head and my beard clean.

Then I returned home and burned all my clothes and all the papers I possessed ... everything! I could not find a shirt for my trip except a traditional Moroccan garment *(jallāba)* that belonged to my brother. I put it on and left, and I kept walking until I reached a river. There I took off my sandals and started walking barefoot with my eyes toward the sky, praying for God to accept my repentance. When I was passing nearby a *souk* the people there started making fun of me. Then I saw the Light fill the horizons, and I thought God was punishing me for my mistakes, and that He would take my sight away. That Light continued to shine and the night sky became as bright as day, but I nevertheless kept walking."

He arrived in Temsaman crying his eyes out, barefoot, his head uncovered. The villagers recognized the young man who had grown up in the *zāwiya*, and they informed Mūlāy al-Ḥasan of what transpired. When Mūlāy al-Ḥasan's son entered in his father's presence, he told him: "I just saw Faouzi walking barefoot with his sandals in his hands." Mūlāy al-Ḥasan retorted, "What is the matter with him? Has he lost his mind?"

Sayyidī Ibn Siniy witnessed the following: "About fifteen minutes later, Sayyidī Shaykh entered and hugged Mūlāy al-Ḥasan's feet, wept profusely, and asked to enter into the spiritual retreat *(khalwa)*. That afternoon, when I was making my *khalwa*, I was with Mūlāy al-Ḥasan in the adjacent room. I heard him cry out the name Allāh, then sob, then cry out again. When he came out of the *khalwa* Mūlāy al-Ḥasan told us that he had been given a great opening (fatḥ).

[Recounting this event,] Sayyidī Shaykh said: "When I went in the presence of Mūlāy al-Ḥasan I found him in the company of the *faqīr* Ibn Siniy in his home, and upon seeing him I threw myself at his feet and hugged them. I told him, 'O my uncle, allow me to enter into the spiritual retreat *(khalwa)*, please.' He kicked me with his feet and said, 'Away from me! You think I let fools like you enter into the spiritual retreat?' Only after having made the spiritual retreat I understood that it was a test. He continued to tell me to get away from him so much so that I decided to leave. On my way out, I heard him say to one of his sons, 'Go accompany him to the taxi station so that he may return home.' I told him, 'No need to. I have been walking for ten years, and now that I want to return towards my Lord, you refuse me, and since God is everywhere I shall depart without return.' Mūlāy al-Ḥasan – may God have mercy upon him – told me, 'And where do you reckon you will go?' I said, 'I will cross the length of the sea until this is over for me.' Witnessing my state, he finally said to me, 'Stay! Go make your ritual ablutions and come.'

I made my ritual ablutions as told. While washing my feet I noticed that they had been soiled with mud and pricked by thorns. When I returned I saw that Mūlāy al-Ḥasan and his children were about to start dining. Mūlāy al-Ḥasan was invoking...

He would stop once in a while to inquire about my parents. Then he called my father and said to him, 'I am jealous of the children that God has bestowed upon you.' This was because Abdel-Nasser, my brother, had also made spiritual retreat *(khalwa)* under the orders of Ḥājj al-Ḥasan, but he had not succeeded in completing it.

When night set in, he came to see me and said, 'Do you prefer to sleep together with my children or alone?' I said, 'I prefer alone.' As I was preparing to go to my room, he told me, 'Wait, wait.' He gave me a small rosary, he held my hand, and then recited some words. Then he said, 'Here, now you have the litany *(wird)*.' I asked him, 'But what should I recite?' He said, 'Wait until tomorrow, I will tell you.' I did not know that this was the oath of allegiance *(bay'a)*. All I desired was to turn to God in repentance *(tawbah)*. I only wanted to be accepted by my Lord. Then I took the Qur'ān that was in the room, looked at the contents and found a *sūrah*, namely *sūrat* al-Tawbah (Chapter 9 of the Qur'ān)... I thought to myself that it was fitting for me who wanted to make *tawbah*.

While reading I noticed that it had no *basmala*,[16] I expected to read verses such as 'My servant, I forgive you,' but no. This *sūrah* was revealed as a disavowal of the unbelievers, and such was my station *(maqām)*.

16 The formula *bismiLlāh al-Rāḥman al-Raḥīm*, "In the Name of God, the Compassionate, the Merciful." The *basmalah* is used at the beginning of each chapter of the Qur'ān with the exception of chapter 9, al-Tawbah (Repentance).

And what a reading ... I didn't even know how to recite the Qur'ān, my reading was arduous, and I would misread every other word... but I succeeded in completing the *sūrah*. I saw myself in every verse that spoke of the unbelievers, and I saw others in the verses regarding Muslims and believers. This is how we read the Qur'ān.

Then I saw the Light. It came from the right and then from the left. Initially I thought it was behind me, then when I kept my sight fixed at a point it would move. Thus I understood that it was a Light coming from within, not from without. I got up in the middle of the night to offer two cycles of prayers and I saw the whole prayer mat become Light."

Sīdī Muḥammad b. Siniy Taibi told us: "We paid a visit to Mūlāy al-Ḥasan for the occasion of Eid al-Fiṭr, the feast of fast-breaking at the end of Ramaḍān.[17] That evening Mūlāy al-Ḥasan gave a *mudhākarah*[18] and was engaged in discussion with his children. We were all paying attention but Sīdī Mohamed Faouzi

17 A Muslim festival marking the ending of the fasting of the month of Ramadan.

18 A short discourse on spiritual matters.

listened with his head down and started to cry. Sīdī Mūlāy al-Ḥasan asked me to perform a spiritual audition *(samā')*, and I did just that. I remember reciting the poem of Sīdī Aḥmad al-'Alāwī – may God sanctify his secret – that begins with *Ayā murīd Allāh n'id lak qawlī asghāh* ("O seeker of God listen to the words I repeat"). That evening it was Sīdī Shaykh who opened the Sufi dance *('imāra).*[19] There were twelve of us present: Mūlāy al-Ḥasan, Sīdī Mohamed Faouzi, Sīdī Muḥammad b. Siniy, Sīdī Mūlāy Ṭayyib (the father), Sīdī Abdel-Nasser, Mounir b. Nourredine, Ṭāhir b. Mūlāy al-Ḥasan, Nourredine b. Mūlāy al-Ḥasan, 'Ādil b. Mūlāy al-Ḥasan, Sa'īd b. Mūlāy al-Ḥasan, Mohamed Amine b. Mūlāy al-Ḥasan, and Ibrahim the young son of Mūlāy al-Ḥasan.

After the Sufi dance *('imāra)*, when the session ended, he sought Mūlāy al-Ḥasan's permission to enter the Path. He told him to wait until his return. I told him to stay with me at Mūlāy al-Ḥasan's place until his return, but he refused. With a disturbed, distraught

19 A synonym for *hadra*, the spiritual dance performed by the Sufis.

look he said: 'I will return, I will return.' And he went back with Mūlāy Ṭayyib to the town of al-Aroui.

"Verily, I have Forgiven You"

Sīdī Mohamed Faouzi al-Karkarī – may God sanctify his secret – said: "The next day, Mūlāy al-Ḥasan came to see me and told me that he would take me into the spiritual retreat *(khalwa)*.

There was no cell for the spiritual retreat *(khalwa)* except for a room that was later turned into a washroom... For indeed, such was my station *(maqām)*, and yet that remains the most precious place for me to this day.

As I was entering into *khalwa* on the fourth day of the month of Shawwāl, Mūlāy al-Ḥasan told me something I shall never forget: "You claim that you wish to know Him who never sleeps? I am old and cannot support your invocation *(dhikr)*,[20] therefore you must not sleep... be sure not to sleep!"

"The fire of repentance that burned in me prevented me from sleeping for three days. When I went to my Shaykh I had nothing. No money, no job, no telephone—absolutely nothing. My head was free from everything, all I had was my body and a traditional Moroccan garment *(jallāba)*.

As I was entering *khalwa*, Mūlāy al-Ḥasan – may God have mercy upon him – asked me to invoke the divine name Allāh, but my only hope was that my Lord would accept my repentance. So I disobeyed him and I only did *istighfār*.[21]

When Mūlāy al-Ḥasan – may God have mercy upon him – saw me do this he said, "Who told you to perform this invocation *(dhikr)*? Invoke the name Allāh. Everything is contained in the name Allāh!" I asked God to show me that He had forgiven me and that He had accepted my repentance. Then I saw in

20 The Shaykh usually continues his *murid's* invocation when the latter falls asleep during *khalwa*.

21 Asking God's forgiveness.

front of me the words 'I have forgiven you' written in letters of Light.

"It was in front of the medium *(wāsiṭa)*[22] that my vision began. I saw the divine name Allāh and, inscribed within it, seven other inscriptions of the name Allāh. For each level I saw a different corresponding verse of the Qur'ān inscribed in letters of Light. I noticed the seven heavens and the earth, from the divine Throne down to the earthly realm, folding up and merging together.

Each folding took place at a different level, and at each level I would see the Qur'ānic verse linked to it as well as its meaning. When Mūlāy al-Ḥasan would come to ask about my state, I would tell him, "O Sayyidī, at this very moment, I see this and that." Whenever I talked to him I was immersed in visions.

He would hear me and start to weep. I was completely drowned in that vision which I beheld all around me.

22 A support on which the Name Allah is written in order to help the disciple in visualizing the letters of the Name. Depending on the context, it may refer to the notion of "intermediary", such as the Shaykh.

"I saw myself becoming a star and then I traveled around the world. While I was in that state Mūlāy al-Ḥasan entered the room and did not find anyone. He went looking for me in the ablution halls but still could see no one. When I came out of the spiritual retreat he asked me where had I gone, and I told him that I had not moved at all.

"My intention was to repent, but God accomplished His greater plan and honored me with His beneficence. In my blessed retreat I saw what no eye has seen, I heard what no ear has heard. The next day, I had my grand spiritual opening and divine replenishment. It was on Friday that God, the Bestower *(al-Wahhāb)*, summoned me to Him and taught me His hidden supreme Name. It was at that moment that I understood who I was, what the meaning of this world is, who my parents are, who my grandparents were, and what the human condition is.

"After two days in the retreat, Mūlāy al-Ḥasan came to find us and wrote the name Allāh with his index finger, saying, "Here is the *Hā'*, here is the *Lām*, another *Lām*, and the *Alif*." He unveiled the inmost secret to us and told us that we must leave the *khalwa*.

We refused; how could one leave such divine favor? We imagined that after the retreat everything that we had witnessed would disappear...He let us stay for another day, after which we came out from the *khalwa*."

Rapture and Wayfaring

When Sīdī Mohamed Faouzi al-Karkarī came out of the spiritual retreat he was enraptured by the divine secret. He broke with his habits and dedicated himself to numerous spiritual practices. He believed that all men possessed knowledge of the secret, except for himself. When he would walk in the marketplace and hear love songs coming from the street vendors, he would weep, feeling that they were songs dedicated to the Lord. He spent the first eight days after his blessed retreat in invocation without leaving his place.

When his spiritual state intensified, he took to the streets, walking on the road's white lines, despite the cars honking, with open arms like a tightrope walker. He would get lost in the vision of the Light, wherefrom he would come out after walking in the middle of the road for miles.

He would wake up around midnight in order to seclude himself in a room and invoke until mid-morning *(ḍuḥā)*.[23] Everybody noticed a complete transformation, as if the former young man had wholly disappeared, and thus the signs of sanctity became visible in him. Sayyidī Abdel-Nasser said: "He would put on the nicest clothes, and then on the day after the *khalwa* he would let his beard grow and put on a traditional Moroccan garment *(jallāba)*. Our mother was astonished at his dedication to the invocation of God... He would come to my workshop every day and lock himself in a small room. There he would invoke from morning to night while constantly fasting, and coming out only for prayers. We would attend the prayers together at al-Aroui's central mosque and then return to the workshop. In the evening, after the evening prayers he would sit and recite the Qur'ān with others in the same mosque, say his litany *(wird)*, and then go home to his family. Sometimes, when

23 A supererogatory prayer, offered when the morning heat is intense and the sun is high in the sky.

Mūlāy al-Ḥasan was passing through al-Aroui, he would come to visit him and would lock himself in my small store with him for thirty to forty minutes."

He fasted for many days, breaking his fast only with soil and water, and in some cases he interrupted his supererogatory fast a few moments before the evening prayer *(maghrib)*. When asked about the reason, he would answer: "Fasting is for God, not for the reward." Sometimes he would sit under the scorching summer sun and invoke his Lord until sunset. He would climb mountains with the intention of leaving only at an order coming directly from God. He said, "Sometimes I would spend an entire day waiting for an order through a voice *(hātif)*,[24] and I would leave only at its occurrence."

Mūlāy Muḥammad b. Siniy Ṭaibi said: "After his spiritual retreat he changed completely. Before, he would laugh and joke from time to time, but after the retreat he was constantly in a state of remembrance, discretion, and modesty. Mūlāy al-Ḥasan would tell

24 Unveiling through audition.

us about him, "Here is a true disciple *(murīd)*. Should you come across others like him send them to me."

For almost six months he visited Sīdī ʿAlī Mūsā's tomb daily, sitting by the tomb and asking God to unveil to him what lied underneath. He recounted to us, "I would go every day, whether it was snowy, windy, or rainy, to a different tomb with the intention of perceiving what lied underneath it. My goal was not to receive an evidentiary miracle or to tempt the Real. Rather, I wished to appease my heart by receiving a physical proof that my Lord had accepted me. I would leave my house before sunrise and return after sunset. Six months passed, and some persons upon seeing me in this state imagined that I was mourning for a family member and sympathized with me. At the end of the sixth month I looked at the sky and saw a tomb being lifted and opened in front of my eyes, and I could see what it contained."[25]

25 When God willed that we (the author) went for *dhikr* at the cemetery of Sīdī Ali Musa, He enabled us to meet its janitor who remembered Sīdī Mohamed Faouzi al-Karkarī. Thus, we received numerous testimonies from persons who had seen him in this state during those six months.

Witnessing the intensity of his state Mūlāy al-Ḥasan called him to hear his news, and when Sayyidī Mohamed Faouzi recounted his unveilings he ordered him to stop all forms of invocation lest he lose his mind. Sayyidī Shaykh Mohamed Faouzi al-Karkarī – may God sanctify his secret – would later say, "It was the only time I disobeyed my master." He performed so much invocation that his tongue was soar.

He said, "When a new clothing item was offered to us we would pray two units in order to see whether it would affect our soul, and if such was the case we would give it away on the first opportunity."

Having been extinguished in his Shaykh, he said: "I loved him as I loved no one before." He told us, "When I would leave to go to him for a question I had, I would reformulate it while walking, and when I would reach there I would be unable to utter my question out of modesty. I would enter his place disappointed after having walked 80 km, but by the grace of God I would receive the response I had sought, through unveiling.

Likewise, as was the practice of the Companions of the Prophet ﷺ, I always waited for the arrival of my Bedouin.[26] In fact, when Mūlāy al-Ḥasan replied to that man, he replied to all my questions, and I was happy ... not with the given replies but with the fact that there existed a definite link between us.

One day when I was visiting him, I saw him browse through a booklet of no more than 15 pages. When he put it down my eyes gazed at it for a few moments. The booklet had no title, no author, nor words, just numbers ... dozens of combinations of numbers. Noticing my interest my Shaykh took it in his hands and said, 'Do you know what it is about? These numbers enable one to calculate the lunar months. Moreover, this booklet has been authored by someone so pious that he did not even write his name, he wrote it only for the sake of God.' I had not understood anything until then, but a single sentence explained everything to me. That booklet is now with me but I have no recollection of how I received it. God knows best. My successor, in turn, will receive the same booklet, inherited from Shaykh to Shaykh. And who is the

26 Someone with no decorum, who has no inhibition to ask questions.

author? God knows best. But I tell you, you shall not find it in any bookstore or library."

Moreover, Mūlāy al-Ḥasan continued to submit his young disciple to numerous trials in order to test his sincerity.[27]

Sīdī Muṣṭafā al-Ribāṭī told us once, "When Sayyidī Shaykh was still being trained by Mūlāy al-Ḥasan I met him in al-Aroui, his lips constantly moving in invocation. He had a traditional Moroccan garment *(jallāba)* which he offered to me by saying, "Take it, so that you may invoke God from underneath it." We used to get together with some *Sharīfs*[28] for *dhikr*. Sayyidī Shaykh joined us in one of our sessions. We were there to show off, to see and be seen, but he had sat at the end in front of the shoe rack, his head lowered, talking to no one, and weeping. When I saw him in that state I understood that he would become a Shaykh."

27 E.g. when Sīdī Mohamed Faouzi showed his poems to him, Mūlāy al-Ḥasan burned them.

28 Descendants of Sīdī b. Qaddūr al-Wakīlī.

Sīdī Idrīs al-Ribāṭī added, "During one of our *dhikr* sessions he wept while his hand did not stop shaking, as if he was trying to contain his spiritual state."

Sayyidī Shaykh Mohamed Faouzi al-Karkarī – may God sanctify his secret – says, "When I came out of the *khalwa* our Shaykh, may God embrace him in His mercy, advised us to read only two books: Ibn 'Aṭā' Allāh al-Iskandarī's aphorisms (Ḥikam) and Shaykh Aḥmad al-'Alāwī's collection of poems, may God be pleased with them. We paid such attention to the words of our Shaykh that we had but three books for our wayfaring… the Book of God, the collection of poems, and the Aphorisms.

Having no other space for spiritual retreat, we would go to our brother's working place. At the back of his shop there was a room that could be locked with a key. It was there that we read the Ḥikam after making our ritual ablutions and sitting in the direction of the *qibla*. We did not just read them, but we also took notes of the levels of meaning that revealed themselves to us while reading. We would continue with a new aphorism of al-Iskandarī *(ḥikma)* only after having applied the present one to our own soul.

We did our best to conform to the particular aphorism *(ḥikma)* that we were reading, which sometimes required several weeks, and sometimes a few days... its application being foremost in our concerns. We remained in that state for several weeks during which we considered the aphorisms of al-Iskandarī as our own friend, and what a friend! With the fire of love still in us, we then read the poems of Shaykh Aḥmad al-ʿAlāwī, may God sanctify his secret.

Many weeks passed in this way until the day when we came across an aphorism of al-Iskandarī that astonished us, and which we shall never forget. It was an aphorism expounding on the true meaning of trust in God *(tawakkul)*. The example provided was that of *Sayyidunā* Ibrāhīm, peace be upon him, when he was hurled in the fire after refusing an angel's help and submitting entirely to his Lord. We were seized by a spiritual state and at that very moment we emptied our pockets from anything that was found in them, and then left with the firm intention of knowing and experiencing trust in God *(tawakkul)*.

We fasted during the day and spent our nights at the cemetery invoking our Lord. During our first period of pious roaming *(siyāḥa)* which lasted ten years we would beg in the streets whenever we had no food, but during this second period of *siyāḥa* we would ask God to feed us, and we took an oath that we would eat only what came directly from Him. If we could not find food until after the evening prayers *(maghrib)* we would lick our fingers to break the fast, and we would mix our saliva with the dust under our feet before swallowing it. We suffered from hunger and cold weather for several days. Do not think that we had no doubts in our souls. Quite the opposite, we would ask ourselves, "Who could feed us, where could we sleep?" But every single time we would turn to our Lord.

We would ask Him to provide for our needs. This went on for several months, until God allowed us to be in such a state that if we wished for a *dirham* we would find it before us. If we wished for bread, we would find it on the ground.

We prayed in submission to God to reveal to us how was this possible? Perhaps the earth was being transformed into money? Perhaps it fell from heaven? God granted our wish.

Once, while we were coming out of the mosque after the late afternoon prayers *(ʿaṣr)* we saw a merchant counting his money. Then as if by miracle one of his bills came out of his batch, it was lifted into the sky, and then it landed right in front of us. We took it in order to return it to the trader. After counting the bills in his batch, he swore to us that none was missing. We swore to him that we had seen that bill getting out of his batch, but he could not understand it.

After about a day in this state we returned to our brother's shop to read the aphorisms of al-Iskandarī. Naïve as we were, we imagined that when Imām Ibn ʿAṭāʾ Allāh al-Iskandarī spoke of the mirror of the heart, he meant an actual mirror. We thought that since the word mirror was used it meant that a particular secret lay hidden behind this. Then we sat in front of a mirror and started invoking the Supreme Name (Allāh) with the firm intention of disappearing from the mirror. We did this for many days until we completely disappeared therefrom. We had no reflection, and when we looked at our bodies it was as if they had become invisible. We looked at the wall behind our backs, and it was as if we had become an eye without a body. Therefore, we thought, if we no longer have a body why not enter into the mirror? Upon entering into the mirror we attained to comprehensions which are impossible for us to express... All of this originated in a lack of comprehension but God judged our good intention and granted our wish. Pay heed, therefore, when I tell you that God is good and that His bounty has no limit; that He is beautiful, and His beauty cannot be contained. How could one not love Him?"[29]

Among the spiritual exercises which he underwent was that he did not stop his fasting for ten days except with dates and pomegranates, then he fasted another ten days interrupting his fast only with water, and finally he completed another ten days without water and food, breaking his fast with invocation from evening *(maghrib)* until the break of dawn *(fajr)*.

Once, while reading the Qur'ān and meditating upon its meanings, he focused on the dot of the letter

29 During this second *siyaha*, he carried only one clothing item which had become coarse and worn out by the time of his return.

qāf (ڡ)[30], and from that dot there appeared a youth named Abdullah. Abdullah grabbed Sayyidī Shaykh's rosary *(subḥa)* and started running around the table. Sayyidī Shaykh got up and followed him until he entered in the dot of the letter *qāf* (ڡ). Upon entering the dot, Sayyidī Shaykh saw a new universe but nevertheless continued to chase Abdullah. When the youth stopped, he stretched his hand and made the rosary beads fly upwards. Sayyidī Shaykh said, "This is an opening to a dimension which I cannot express. After gathering the rosary beads, I decided to return to the physical realm. Little by little, like a film rewinding, I emerged from the dot, then I made a circle around the table and reentered my body. I took the Qur'ān and showed it to my brother, asking him to check the dot in order to verify whether he was seeing what I was seeing."

He says, "During my wayfaring, I exerted myself in continuous self-examination *(murāqaba)*.[31] One

30 In the old North African Arabic script, the consonant *Qāf* has one, not two dots (ڡ), while the letter *Fā'* is written with a dot beneath the line.

31 Constant connection of the heart with the Lord.

night when I was sleeping the devil tempted me to commit a reprehensible act in my dream. I became aware immediately, and by the grace of God, I was able to thwart his plot. When I woke up, I saw him in front of me. Instead of being afraid or jumping, I stood still to observe him. I saw him change from form to form. This is how I recognized the twelve different forms of the devil."

When he would invoke his Lord he would be so absent from this world that he would not notice what was in front of him. Once, he told me, "Sometimes it is truly difficult to come out of the spiritual world and return to the realm of forgetfulness *(ghafla)*." I also heard him say, "Just as every wayfarer exerts himself greatly to burn the world around him, the realized man must make a considerable effort to bring it back." How many times did I enter in the presence of Sayyidī Shaykh while he was holding his rosary in his hand, and it was as if he did not see me.

Very quickly, the saintly miracles that are characteristic of the saints of the Muḥammadan community began to manifest themselves through Sīdī Mohamed Faouzi. He said, "When God taught me the science of spiritual vision I became capable of lifting gas cylinders only with the help of my sight. In order to convince me that what I was seeing was true I lifted the gas cylinders to a certain height and let it go. When it fell, the impact made a hole on the ground."

During his wayfaring under the aegis of Mūlāy al-Ḥasan, Sīdī Shaykh Mohamed Faouzi al-Karkarī – may God sanctify his secret – would offer his Friday prayers at al-Aroui's central mosque. He says, "When Mūlāy al-Ḥasan was still alive we would go to al-Aroui's central mosque. When the Imām would deliver his sermon we would become absent from ourselves. The mosque walls were covered in tiles. We would lift tiles through vision in the state of wakefulness and see the Divine Name hidden underneath. Then we would put the tile down nearby. Then, we would lift a second tile and discover another Divine name hidden underneath. This is how we learned that the divine names stood opposite to each other and that they were correlated. Towards the end of the sermon all the walls of the mosque were covered by the Divine Name written in Light. When the Imām began the closing invocation, we hurried to put all the tiles back one by one until the wall regained its original form. When we reached the status of spiritual guide we learned that the mosque had been levelled to the ground, perhaps due to that incident. And God knows best."

Among the unveilings granted to our Shaykh while wayfaring under the care of his Shaykh was the following incident, which he related to us: "When our Shaykh was still alive, in one of the invocation sessions *(dhikr)* I saw my own image emerging from myself, just as you see me now. Then I exerted myself in invocation for several days until a second image in my likeness emerged from that image. This went on until I saw a whole gathering of persons in my likeness. The next step was to make them invoke, and these images started invoking, and after a few days, I succeeded. The space in which we had gathered was filled with invocation. Then I began to give a particular invocation and color to each of those images. Finally, I had an invocation session during my own spiritual retreat wherein each image had its own invocation and clothes. This is the reason why they say that the knower of God is never alone. To find out whether my *dhikr* had reached the physical realm, I asked all the images to leave the room. They all got up and left, and they closed the door behind. When I finished my invocation, I stood up and noticed that the door was open. Hence I understood that the vision had had an effect in the physical world."

Innumerable sciences descended upon his heart,[32] making him a receptacle of divine knowledge.

32 He told us, "One evening I could study almost 60 Divine Names."

Divine Permission *(idhn)*

Given the excellence of his manners, as well as his mastery of the Path, Sayyidī Mohamed Faouzi received from Mūlāy al-Ḥasan the permission *(idhn)* to transmit various invocations of the Path and to connect the wayfarers to the Path. However, he refused to transmit the litany *(wird)* while his Shaykh was alive. Whenever someone asked him to join the Path, he directed him to Mūlāy al-Ḥasan. This was due to his modesty and his love towards his Shaykh.

After some time he received permission to train disciples *(tarbiyya)*. He says, "It was in the house of our Shaykh, in Temsamam, that we were granted permission to assume the status of spiritual master *(mashayakha).*[33] That evening we saw the whole creation giving us the oath of allegiance. We did not relate our visions to our Shaykh but ever since that night he did not stop praising *(yuzakkīnā)* us in the eyes of people."

Thus, Sīdī Abdel-Nasser said, "I heard Mūlāy al-Ḥasan praise Sayyidī Shaykh in four occasions. The first was during a telephone call with Sīdī b. Siniy, in which Mūlāy al-Ḥasan said, 'He is an authorized functionary in the order *(muqaddam)*, he may transmit the litany *(wird)*.' The second time, Mūlāy al-Ḥasan said in my presence, 'He is one of the friends of God *(awliyā' Allāh)*.' On the third time, I heard him say, "Beware of contradicting him, he is a spiritual Pole *(quṭb)*." And on the fourth time he said, 'Whatever is found here (pointing towards his heart) is found there (pointing towards Sīdī Mohamed Faouzi's heart).'"

On another occasion, he gave him full authorization. This occurred when the father of our Shaykh, Sīdī Tayyib, the brother of Mūlāy al-Ḥasan, told him, "Why don't you give Sīdī Mohamed an authorization

33 The function of the Shaykh.

so that people benefit from him?" Mūlāy al-Ḥasan replied, "Rather, he does have an authorization that has been given to him some time ago."

Sīdī Muḥammad b. Siniy Taibi says, "We were in a car with Sīdī Mohamed Faouzi, Mūlāy al-Ḥasan, and Sīdī Mūlāy Ṭayyib when Mūlāy al-Ḥasan said to Sīdī Mohamed Faouzi, 'You shall become a Pole.'" *the greatest living saint of an age*

After a short time, Sīdī Mohamed Faouzi had a vision announcing the approaching death of Mūlāy al-Ḥasan. Out of modesty, he decided not to relate his vision but during a visit, Mūlāy al-Ḥasan asked him about what he had seen. While he was relating his vision, Mūlāy al-Ḥasan said, "God willing, it shall be so."

When the pangs of death seized Mūlāy al-Ḥasan,[34] his entire family, his relatives, and his children as well as Sayyidī Mohamed Faouzi gathered around him. Sayyidī Shaykh told me, "A lady from our family did not agree for us take him to the doctor. She had been present in many such occasions before and knew when the time had come. I only hoped one

---

34 Mūlāy al-Ḥasan joined the greatest Companion in ٢٠٠٦.

thing, to die instead of him, or with him. In order to relieve him I applied water to his face. He repeated the singular divine name *(al-ism al-mufrad)*, 'Allāh... Allāh...Allāh.' I stood up and held his right hand with my left hand, to help him pronounce the testimony of faith (*shahāda*). At that very moment, all family members left the room, with the exception of one person, *lalla* Soumaya, and an old blind uncle. I was alone with him, my hands above his. This is how he breathed his last. When his spirit left him, a mysterious thing occurred which shall remain between him and myself."[35]

35 I heard Sayyidī Shaykh Mohamed Faouzi al-Karkarī – may God sanctify his secret – say. "The angel of death cannot grasp the spirit of the friend of God (*walī*), it is the inheriting disciple that grasps the spirit of the friend of God (*walī*)."

The Shaykh

When Shaykh Mūlāy al-Ḥasan passed away, our Shaykh inherited the status of the Shaykh of the Path despite the fact that this did not look obvious after Mūlāy al-Ḥasan's death.

Then he reached the highest stations and became a person towards whom all men and jinn seeking guidance were directed, without anyone knowing that he was a Shaykh.

He says, "I attained to a level of nearness and knowledge after the death of my Shaykh that he had not achieved himself during his lifetime." He continued in this way until the Real honored him with the station of Seal *(khatmiya)*, which is in reality the heritage of the divine names and of Muḥammadan Successorship, *(al-khalīfa al-Muḥammadi)*.

He said, "The authorization to become spiritual master *(mashaykha)* was made first by the Shaykh, then by the Prophet ﷺ personally, and then by God." He then added, "We never sought to become a Shaykh, this fell upon us without us desiring it. It is a divine bestowal *(hiba)*."

He said, "The permission *(idhn)* of this Path is from Ibn Mashīsh *(mashīshīyya)*, for among all the *Shaykhs* of the initiatic chain *(silsila)*, the only one to transmit the Light of allegiance *(bay'a)* as we do was Shaykh Mūlāy 'Abd al-Salām Ibn Mashīsh."

He said, "I saw the collectivity of my disciples giving me the oath of allegiance in the spiritual realm, I know them all. I know their beginning, their end, whether they are among the felicitous *(sa'īd)* or the wretched *(shaqī)*, the stations they will occupy, and most incredibly, I still remember each of them." In fact, a man from Belgium wanted to meet our Shaykh during his visit to Europe.

When Sayyidī Shaykh saw him, he told us, "He will not enter the Path, for when a disciple comes to us and we recognize him, our heart starts to quiver." This person visited the Shaykh at the al-Aroui *zāwiya* and left after a week without asking to join the Path. Then we had no news of him.

He said, "On the night of 12 Rabīʿ al-Awwal 2007 I had a vision that made me reach the status of Shaykh. Contrary to what many think, the oath of allegiance *(bayʿa)* is a descent and not an ascent. It descends *(nuzūliyya)* from the Lord to the servant. This vision came about in the sensorial world. I saw myself receiving the oath of allegiance *(bayʿa)* from God, then the Prophet ﷺ took allegiance *(bayʿa)* from me, and then *Sayyidunā* ʿAlī, and then al-Ḥasan and al-Husayn in the presence of their mother, Fāṭima al-Zahrāʾ. Then I saw all the *Shaykhs* of the blessed initiatic tree, one by one, coming to take the oath of allegiance *(bayʿa)* before me. It was while I was passing from one Shaykh to another that the reality of the hidden Supreme Name manifested itself to me. The scene was so terrifying that I escaped. I ran away and refused it. I took flight until I found my Shaykh, Mūlāy al-Ḥasan who took out the rosary of one thousand beads *(subḥa alfiyya)* and made me accept it. Then the Supreme Name and the secret of the Essence appeared. At that very moment hatred was removed from my heart, and there remained nothing but love for the whole of creation. That is the reason why a Shaykh never judges his disciple, even though he may know his lowest thoughts and his basest intentions. Thus, a Shaykh's love outstrips a disciple's love. This is the reason why a Shaykh may initiate and guide a disciple even if he is found in the middle of the ocean, for they have given their allegiance *(bay'a)* to us in the spiritual realm *(malakūt)*."

Sīdī Mohamed Faouzi – may God sanctify his secret – spent a year alone, unknown by anyone, in complete obscurity *(khumūl)*, so much that even his wife knew nothing about his state. She would see him wake up, make the ablutions, sit in the direction of the Ka'ba *(qibla)*, and perform invocation *(dhikr)* for hours. He was looking for someone to share the secrets of the Essence, for when the secret dwells in the heart the tongue cannot remain at rest.

He says, "I prostrated myself and asked Him, 'A single person ... just one... I only ask Thee for a single person that I may converse with him.'"

His mother, *lalla* Yamna, and his brother, Sīdī Abdel-Nasser knew that he had become a Shaykh and that he had received the authorization to transmit the teachings of the Path. Both wanted to join the Path at his hands, but he repeatedly avoided their requests. Sīdī Abdel-Nasser said, "When Mūlāy al-Ḥasan passed away I was afraid of plummeting. I would visit Sīdī Shaykh often and ask him to allow me to join the Path. I continued to ask continuously until one day he gave me the litany *(wird)* which then did not contain chapters from the Qur'ān. Thus I became the first disciple of the Karkariyya branch."

I heard Sayyidī Shaykh say, "My mother asked me to initiate her but out of modesty I avoided responding. How could I be the Shaykh of my own mother? Yet, she had grown up in the *zāwiya* of Mūlāy Ṭāhir, she knew the value of *bay'a*, so she persisted until I initiated her. She died a short time afterwards, with her head on my lap, invoking the Name Allāh."

Sīdī Muḥammad b. Siniy Taibi told us, "After Mūlāy al-Ḥasan's passing I asked his son, Nourredine, if we had to renew the *wird* with him. His response was, "No, the *wird* is that of my father." We had gone to see Sīdī Shaykh Mohamed Faouzi al-Karkarī to ask him if he was a Shaykh. He declined to answer. Each time I would come across him I would ask him if he was a Shaykh, and he would not reply, until one day he told me, 'Yes, I am a Shaykh.'"

A year later came the obligation of calling others to God *(da'wah)*. Were he to refuse, everything would be taken away from him.

He said, "The more a Shaykh desires to remain in obscurity, the greater his outward exposure." When he received the obligation of *da'wah* he said, "I went to the rocks to make *da'wah* to them, but they told me to go to men. Whenever I heard good words about someone I would visit him for *da'wah*." The beginnings were difficult, and he had to tolerate the evil and mockery of many a person. One day, as he was exiting the mosque a wretch appeared who spat on his noble face.

Our Shaykh did not even think of revenge or returning the insult. On the contrary, he wiped his face and continued his way. The first disciples to join our Shaykh were those who had followed Mūlāy al-Ḥasan – may God be pleased with him – in his lifetime, namely our Shaykh's mother, *lalla* Yamna,

Sīdī Abdel-Nasser al-Karkarī, and Sīdī Muḥammad b. Siniy.

Sīdī Abdel-Nasser brought Sīdī Said Menouach to the Path, who was then seventeen. Then it was the turn of Sīdī Ḥājj Muḥammad Fadhil, our Shaykh's wife, *lalla* Najet, Sīdī Aḥmad Boutaba, and Sīdī Aḥmad b. Ṭayyib, our Shaykh's brother.

Sīdī Ḥājj Muḥammad Fadhil told me once, "We had heard that Sayyidī Shaykh had made the spiritual retreat *(khalwa)* with Mūlāy al-Ḥasan, and it was through that retreat that we entered the Path. At the beginning of the Path, when we were only four or five disciples, we used to gather in the dentist office of Sīdī Mūlāy Abdel-Nasser, our Shaykh's brother, and we would spend entire nights and days with him. Whenever the call for prayers would be announced we would go to the mosque, and then return to the office. During the summer, we would gather at the inner courtyard of the marketplace, under a tree, in order to listen to Sayyidī Shaykh's discourses *(mudhākarāt)*.

Without a *zāwiya* and a gathering place, Sīdī Shaykh said, "The first course that we held was a commentary of Shaykh Aḥmad al-ʿAlāwī's poems, followed by a commentary of Imām Ibn ʿAṭāʾ Allāh al-Iskandarī's aphorisms. During almost two years we explained the meanings of the aphorisms to the *fuqarāʾ*. We who did not understand any book became expositors of books... We gave such importance to those two books that after completing their commentary, Shaykh Aḥmad al-ʿAlāwī and Imām Ibn ʿAṭāʾ Allāh al-Iskandarī – may God be pleased with them – came to thank us in person in the spiritual realm *(malakūt)*. Shaykh Aḥmad al-ʿAlāwī then enabled us to visit his *zāwiya* in Mostaghanem, and he showed us how he slaughtered a ram to inaugurate his *zāwiya*, which is why we slaughtered a ram too for the inauguration of our *zāwiya*."

The Path was quite different from what the disciples know today. Upon initiation each of them received one of the sixty-three allusions *(ishārāt)* corresponding to the years of the Prophet's ﷺ lifetime in this world. The contemplation of that spiritual allusion was supposed to lead the disciple to the vision of Light. Only then could he enter into *khalwa*. Sayyidī Shaykh said, "The first four disciples that I put into *khalwa* were all under the spiritual direction of Sīdī al-Ḥasan, and it was he who told me how to proceed with them."

Back then, the room in which most of the disciples now make the *khalwa* had not been constructed yet. The first disciple who made a *khalwa*, Sīdī 'Allāl, had to use a room in Mūlāy Ṭayyib's house.

The first twelve disciples who made the *khalwa* were: Sīdī 'Allāl, Sīdī Abdel-Nasser, Sīdī Ahmed (Sīdī Shaykh's brother), Sīdī Said Menouach, Sīdī Muḥammad b. Siniy Taibi, Sīdī Ḥājj Muḥammad Fadhil, Sīdī Abdel-Hafiz Ribāṭī, *lalla* Najāt, Ḥājj Taieb Chérif alias al-Ouadi, Sīdī Aḥmad Boutaba, Sīdī 'Azīz, and Sīdī Abdel-Hamid. All of them experienced spiritual openings from which they benefited greatly. The Lights of the divine proximity and the brightness of supreme knowledge appeared to them. Sayyidī Shaykh says, "Our Path is one of vision in wakefulness, and whoever does not achieve vision I am not their Shaykh and he is not my disciple." Thus, the Path began to take shape little by little until his fame crossed borders and oceans. Our Shaykh continued to teach the secrets of the Name Allāh in his *zāwiya* which is still located in al-Aroui.

His Character

There are no words to describe his character. However eloquent the words may be they can never depict even an atom of his character and his merits. How can one describe a person who through the nobility of his character sealed the readings of the Name of Majesty; how can one describe a servant whose goal transcended both worlds, whose sight has turned away from everything other than his goal, whom no station encompasses, whom no evidentiary miracle *(karāmah)* distracts, and whose aim is only God, the One? His state is such that whoever keeps his company benefits from the Lights and receives hitherto unexpected insights into his heart. For he quenches the hearts from an indestructible source, the fountain of prophethood, may God enable us to benefit from Him.

Among his qualities is humility. We witnessed the expression of his great humility so that we who are his disciples were captivated on the first occasion. In fact, we saw him innumerous times arranging the shoes of the *fuqarāʾ*. In this lore of Sufism the disciples work and put themselves at the service of spiritual masters, but in the case of our Shaykh it is he who works for the disciples. We saw him with our own eyes, and in several occasions, washing the restrooms for his disciples, cleaning their clothes, and bringing them food. I saw him many times washing the sacrificed cattle's intestines. When the neighbors garbage would pile up he would burn it with his own hands, often spending hours at it, in spite of several illnesses he suffered from. He sought nothing but humility and loathed honorary tributes. He wore a woman's multicolored patched frock *(muraqqaʿa)*, and when he would go out in it my heart would tighten even though I was not the one wearing it. One day I attended a lecture by our noble Shaykh, which was so profound that I thought to myself that his lectures had to reach others so that more people knew about the treasures at our disposal. At that moment Sayyidī Shaykh looked at me and said, "A long time ago the fame of a certain Shaykh had reached the royal court. The king wanted to meet this Shaykh and went to see him. When he arrived, he found an old man grazing the grass... The *shaykhs* do not wish to be recognized in order to be left alone."

Some of his actions will remain in my memory forever. For instance, on the celebration of the Prophet's ﷺ birthday in January 2014 I wanted to sleep in the *zāwiya* to benefit from its blessings. As I was about to fall asleep, I saw Sayyidī Shaykh waiting for me at the door of the *khalwa* room with his arms full of blankets which he had carried from several stores above. Likewise, God allowed me to fast continuously for several days, after which the Shaykh himself brought me a dish for breaking fast. One night the dish was not there, and he gave me his own meal, telling me with a smile, "Tonight you will dine like a Shaykh." Who could show such patience by bringing a dish to his disciple each day for several weeks, except one whom God had showered with His blessings?

He taught us modesty and humility through his own example. He does not discriminate between rich and poor, and in his eyes the powerful is the same as the vagabond. The doors of his *zāwiya* are open to all, day and night, for the devout and the rascal. How many university professors and researchers, as well as men of power, found themselves sitting face to face with illiterates. I heard him address them in the following words, "Stay with us as much as you wish, but here you shall eat from the same plate as the dervishes *(fuqarā')*, and you shall sleep on rugs." Among his traits is compassion towards all creatures, be they humans or animals. He suffers and gets upset from the situation of his disciple who is undergoing trials, and he is happy when good befalls him. As far as God's rights are concerned, he fears nobody's blame, in spite of the violence and attacks against him. On day he said, "We throw Light at people, and they throw fire at us." His magnanimity is such that many disciples were hostile to the Path before their breasts were expanded to the Light of God, but once God put the love for the Shaykh in their hearts, they no longer had any animosity. Likewise, when the

Karkariyya branch began to spread, Mūlāy al-Ḥasan's children started attacking and slandering our Shaykh, claiming that they were the true heirs of their father's secret. Our Shaykh did not respond to any of their attacks. He told us, "I ask you not to respond to them. Out of my respect and love for my Shaykh I will not respond to them."

Among his qualities are generosity and kindness. They manifest themselves in their fullest breadth and in their noblest degree in the fact that he gives Light to his disciples and leads them to spiritual secrets. A true Shaykh is only one who gives his secret away. And a true Shaykh is one who gives his Light away. There are no words to describe his greatness and his generosity. He told us, "When a beggar stretches his hand give him whatever you have, and if you give him only your small change know that you expose your station *(maqām)*."

Among the adorning qualities are faithfulness and integrity. He covers his disciple with the veil of compassion, while knowing perfectly his inner state, and he never reveals his faults or disowns him. I have heard him say about someone who attacked the spiritual Path, "By God, I love him." He says, "A Shaykh never disowns his disciple, rather, it is the disciple that turns away from the Shaykh."

Also, our brother in God, Sīdī Muḥammad Pierre came to see our Shaykh to present a letter to him. Sayyidī Shaykh asked me to translate the letter for him. The brother in question, having seen his heart be filled with the Light of certitude, had decided to offer the Shaykh all he possessed, his property, his car, etc. For this purpose, he had signed and sealed a notarized donation act. When Sayyidī Shaykh saw it, he took the letter in his hand and told Pierre, "Know that I accept your gift, but allow me..." He took the donation act and tore it to little pieces, which he placed in an envelope, and then said, "I will keep your letter and hope to be buried with it." He wears the dress of poverty. Everything he receives he gives to feed the disciples in the *zāwiya*.

It is impossible for me to relate the number of anecdotes about his state and his generosity, both of which I witnessed in his blessed presence. That is due to his having walked through all divine realms wherein he realized that everything comes from God. I accompanied him for a long time. He made me understand the perfection of his character, and he captivated me with the beauty of his comportment. He has acquired these traits in their perfection. That is the reason why God has chosen his heart as a receptacle for His sacred secret. Truly, I have never seen anyone who combines in himself so many qualities in their perfection as Sayyidī Shaykh does, may God increase his nobility.

His Knowledge

He has mastered the totality of sciences and gnosis, thereby becoming the heir of the seal *(khatmiyya)* of the hidden Supreme Name. He says, "The particularity of the seal of saints *(khatm)* is that you will find him superior in all domains of knowledge; whichever science you investigate, you will find that he outstrips you therein." He unveils the sciences only to deserving hearts, after having tried them. His knowledge is received through unveiling, and when the disciple succeeds in achieving knowledge through the invocation *(dhikr)* he discovers that the heart of his noble Shaykh is an endless ocean of knowledge and sciences. Among the sciences which I was allowed to discover in the heart of our Shaykh and which he transmitted to me through unveiling are the science of the divination (*ʿilm al-jafr*), astrology, the science of physiognomy, and the science of the lunar phases. He shares his science with his disciples, each of whom reveals a facet of his knowledge. Some disciples study the sciences of the Syriac figures and letters, while others study the science of the Divine Names. His heart is an ocean of secrets. He says, "Take from me whatever you wish. My science stems from the Messenger of God. How much can you retain, O disciple, from the divine lights and mysteries? And yet, I never grow tired... so long as you do not grow tired!"

While limiting himself to the realm of the senses, his speech is lofty and subdues the intellects. How many university graduates have I seen who were astonished at his knowledge. He expresses himself on a wide range of subjects with great accuracy, whether it be the sciences of the Law or profane sciences. While I was attending one his courses, a few days after being initiated, I asked him on the origin of his knowledge, and he told me, 'I have learned everything in my *khalwa*, I have only read a couple of books'..."

He, may God enable us to benefit from him, makes the great come from the small. This is a characteristic of the Folk of God. For example, our Shaykh Mohamed Faouzi al-Karkarī spent ten years in explaining the secrets contained in the letter *Hā'* of the Majestic Name. Likewise, I heard him hold a thirty-session commentary on the Chapter The Cave of the Qur'ān, and on the poems of Shaykh al-'Alāwī. In each session, he brought a new understanding and new subtleties to the commentary. He tells us often, "I turn the pages quickly. If you want to stop at each page, no one will pass beyond the first secret."

This is a clear indication of his generosity and of his eagerness to facilitate the Path for the disciple. He carries him from one station to another with relatively little effort, within a brief time, so that the dervish does not become aware of the station that he passes. If he speaks about a handful of Light and its manifestations, it will suffice to grasp the fragrance of its distinctiveness. If he speaks about the Names and their manifestations, the heart becomes inebriated by the exhilaration of proximity and sanctity. If he speaks of the elect, the heart is filled with the manifested Light.

This is how Light enters the heart. As for his own state, it is like speaking about an exuberant sea or a firm mountain. In fact, he is constantly witnessing the Living, the Worshiped. Since he knows the Real he is no longer veiled from Him. The Messenger of God ﷺ is always present with his vision. I have heard him say, "By God, if the Messenger of God were veiled from me for an instant I would not count myself among the Muslims." On the contrary, one finds among his disciples those who experience the same state. What should be the state of the master from whom they acquire this, then? The disciple, whatever his degree of proximity may be, cannot know the true value of this peerless guide. If he wants to give to you he gives, and if he wants to deprive you, he deprives you. When he speaks he embraces all hearts, and everyone benefits from his words, be they novices, adepts, or among those who have attained.

His Physical Appearance

Sayyidī 'Abd al-Ḥafīẓ al-Ribāṭī says while describing our Shaykh's physical appearance, "He is neither big nor small. He has fair skin and a handsome face. His eyes contain an astonishing liveliness. His look is piercing. It often happens that our eyes meet and I feel a shiver. It has happened many times that our eyes interlock, and I feel a shivering in my body. Sometimes this shivering reaches my eyes and tears come down my face. His face contains a Light which cannot go unnoticed by those gifted with insight. Whoever sees him feels awe, and whoever visits him loves him. He has abandoned chosen clothes for the patched frock *(muraqqa'a)*."

I say, he has an aquiline nose, which is round and big. His black beard is tinted in grey and rather thick.

His joints are strong but his body remains harmonious and well proportioned. Whoever sees him will perceive the loveliness that emerges from his face as well as his voice, which is at once soft and strong, an almost androgynous voice.

His Worship and Exertion

In this domain he follows in the footsteps of the Prophet ﷺ, never deviating from his example. He has made the words of the Prophet ﷺ his life's compass, and each of his daily actions are inspired by them. He performs all types of worship. At times, I have heard him invoke his Lord in tears during the whole night, and at times he invokes for an hour before the morning prayers *(fajr)*. Sometimes he fasts uninterruptedly, and sometimes he breaks his fast. He has never imposed the smallest duty upon a disciple without performing it himself first. He says, "When the authorization descends, I obligate myself with it for a full lunar year before imposing it on a disciple." His worship is characterized by constancy. He keeps night vigils with *dhikr*, followed by the morning prayers and litanies *(awrād)* until sunrise *(shurūq)*. He gets up after *ḍuḥā* and sits outside of the *zāwiya*, whether it is rainy or windy, to read the Qur'ān for several hours until mid-day prayers *(ẓuhr)*, completing several full readings of the Book each month. Then he offers the late afternoon *('aṣr)* and evening *(maghrib)* prayers. Whenever he is not holding a class, he continues his invocation alone. We have heard him many times invoking *(dhikr)* for several hours at the *zāwiya*.

Among his acts of worship are vigils during the Night of Power *(Laylat al-qadr)* and the night of 15th of the month of Sha'bān, when he stays with his wife and children in his apartment to remember God, making the *zāwiya* reverberate with divine invocations. Likewise, during festival days he takes out the thousand beads rosary *(subḥa alfiyya)*, and spends several days in invocation surrounded by his disciples. One of the most remarkable images that I have seen in the presence of this noble Shaykh was his supplication during the Prophet's ﷺ birthday *(mawlid)* in 2016. After sitting, he raised his arms and started to invoke God. His invocation lasted for almost three hours, and several of his disciples left the place. A few moments before the morning prayers, when only a handful disciples were left around him, he got up and continued to pray until the call to prayer was heard.

He says, "The seeker should exert himself in all actions of worship. Sometimes he must keep vigil all night long, and at other times half of the night. Sometimes he should fast uninterruptedly, and on other days he must fast and then break his fast. He must travel in the kingdom of God on foot, going to Him without money or luggage in order to achieve trust in God *(tawakkul)*. That is how a seeker should be, so that if he is guided to God he will have tasted everything. If he speaks of asceticism, or trust in God, or isolation and retreat, he will have experienced them himself." He says, "Whatever I have obtained was through isolation and travel."

His Saintly Miracles

It is impossible to list the totality of his saintly miracles owing to their great number. Such is his saintly aspiration *(himma)* that his own disciples are subject to saintly miracles. He says, "You will never hear me speak of my unveilings, for it is enough for me to ask a disciple to relate his visions in order to captivate the intellects." And as our master Sayyidī Aḥmad al-ʿAlāwī says, "A Shaykh's saintly aspiration manifests in his disciple."

The greatest saintly miracle is granted to those who possess uprightness *(istiqāma)* and follow the Messenger of God in all states, both inward and outward. Nevertheless, we will quote some of the saintly miracles that we have witnessed in the presence of our blessed Shaykh.

Among his most remarkable saintly miracles is the descending of the divine Light upon the heart of his disciples in order to make him accede to direct witnessing, even at the moment of initiation. He says, "Our Path is one of direct witnessing in a state of wakefulness. Whoever does not directly witness, I am not his master and they he is not my disciple." Whoever embarks upon the Path is thrown into the holy presence of the Attribute of Light. What greater miracle is there than making a divine attribute descend upon the heart of someone, regarding which He has said, "**God is the Light of the heavens and the earth. The parable of His Light is a niche, wherein is a lamp. The lamp is in a glass. The glass is as a shining star kindled from a blessed olive tree, neither of the East nor of the West. Its oil would well-nigh shine forth, even if no fire had touched it. Light upon light. God guides unto His Light whomsoever He will, and God sets forth parables for mankind, and God is Knower of all things.**"[36]

36 Qur'ān, 24:35 (trans. *The Study Quran*).

Not only does this noble Shaykh transmit the divine Light at the moment of initiation, but also to disciples living in distant regions, without having met them physically. In fact, numerous persons living in war-torn countries such as Iraq and Syria, cannot travel to Morocco to be initiated. Such disciples are initiated through the telephone after having made the *wird* for forty days, and all of them bear witness to the vision of Light. Likewise, I have heard Sayyidī Shaykh Mohamed Faouzi, may God sanctify his secret, say, "Whoever desires to take the oath of allegiance *(bay'a)* sincerely let him wake up in the last third of the night, make his ablutions, and after offering two units of prayers let him raise his right hand and say, 'O God, I pledge allegiance from Shaykh Mohamed Faouzi al-Karkarī. I recognize him as The friend of God of his age.' If his intention is pure he will receive the Light, because he is living during the time of the "master of his age' *(ṣāḥib al-waqt)*. In this manner, hundreds of disciples are able to contemplate the Light in a wakeful state, without having ever met the Shaykh. Some of them have even been able to make *khalwa* and attain to the secret of the Essence from afar. For indeed, how can one who has been extinguished in the Light, burning away the limitations of space and time, find himself limited?

Among his saintly miracles is his capacity to appear in different locations simultaneously. We have witnessed this in several occasions, such as receiving Sayyidī Shaykh for a visit, while we were in Belgium. Likewise, when Sayyidī Shaykh initiated a disciple who was imprisoned in the United States, the detainee told him, "I see you with me." Sayyidī Shaykh's response was, "You will realize that I am always with you."

His unveiling is so intense that the smallest thoughts and intentions of others are present before him. During his discourses *(mudhārakarāt)*, he unveils and describes a disciple's inner state in such an elegant and refined manner that the disciple recognizes himself.

Then he guides him and advises him without anyone realizing the person intended. In this way, he covers the faults of a disciple while guiding him. The immensity of his unveiling is known to all of his disciples.

During November 2016, a few days after the blessed Prophet's birthday *(mawlid)*, about forty disciples had gathered at the *zāwiya* in al-Aroui. One evening, Sayyidī Shaykh Mohamed Faouzi al-Karkarī – may God sanctify his secret – told us during a discourse *(mudhākara)*, "There is one among you who has come here to acquire vision of the Light. However, when he left his house he lied to his family that he was going to Casablanca (lit. white house).[37] Well, this is indeed a white house, that is, a house of Light. But when he uttered it, his intention was different. If he recognizes himself and confesses his lie before everyone, he will return with a gushing light in his heart."

After some moments of silence, an Algerian disciple raised his hand and said, "Sīdī, I told my family that I was going to Spain." Then, another disciple confessed that he had lied to his family, "I told them that I was going to such and such country." Several disciples recognized their faults similarly, but Sayyidī Shaykh told them, "No, it is none of you. I am speaking about a son of this country, so let him reveal himself. I prom-

37 The city of Casablanca, Spanish for white house.

ise to him Light in exchange." Several minutes passed before a brother from the town of al-Hoceima raised his hand and said, "Yes Sīdī, I did lie to my parents that I was going to Casablanca, so that they would not worry." Sayyidī Shaykh smiled and said, "Yes, I meant you. Now rectify your intention and here is the Light." Then he acquired vision of the Light. We were about forty disciples in the same room, and many can testify to this scene—and all praise belongs to God.

In 2016, a group of Algerian brothers from Mostaghanem came to see our Shaykh – may God sanctify his secret – in his *zāwiya* of al-Aroui. Some of them, upon seeing the humility and modesty of our Shaykh who was dressed in a patched frock *(muraqqa'a)* which few could carry, and used as they were to masters wearing the finest clothes, they started doubting our Shaykh. One day, Shaykh Mohamed Faouzi al-Karkarī, may God sanctify his secret, held a discourse *(mudhākarah)* during which he unveiled the minutest thoughts of the Algerian brothers. Then, when he finished he struck the low table before getting up, and silence fell in the *zāwiya*. Just before leaving, Sayyidī Shaykh turned and said to one of the Algerians, "You, tell them what you just saw!" He replied, "Sīdī, at the moment when you struck the table I saw galaxies and stars appearing." Sayyidī Shaykh looked at the other Algerians and told them, "Your brother came with sincerity, and within a few moments he was illuminated!" When he left, no one dared make the smallest gesture. I went downstairs and saw Sayyidī Shaykh smiling, and he said to me, "You see, sometimes sticks can be useful too." Afterwards all the Algerians were initiated, and they embarked on the Path. They opened the first Karkariyya *zāwiya* in Mostghanem, the city which had welcomed the Shaykh of our *shaykhs*, Sīdī Aḥmad al-ʿAlāwī, may God sanctify his secret.

Two years later, one of the brothers who were present at this incident was still unable to attain to the vision of the Light. Sayyidī Shaykh said during a discourse *(mudhākara)* held on the *mawlid* of November 2018, "Whoever among you has seen the Light, let him raise his hand." All the disciples raised their hands. Sayyidī Shaykh said, "You! Do not raise your hand for you have not seen it. Do you know why? Do you remember when I struck the table while you were talking on the phone to another Shaykh? At that very moment the heart of your brother was illuminated whereas your heart was extinguished. After this discourse, go to the room downstairs, offer two units of prayer, and converse with your Lord. You shall see the Light, by the grace of God." This is what the brother did, and he saw the Light.

Sīdī Mohamed al-Hebri, a disciple of noble lineage, was invoking in the city of Oujda with the help of a rosary *(subḥa)* which he held in his hand. During his invocation God granted him with a vision during which he felt that the rosary slip from his hand. He continued his *dhikr* as if nothing had happened. When he finally finished, he noted that the rosary had disappeared. A few days later he went to an invocation session led by Sīdī Mohamed Faouzi al-Karkarī, may God sanctify his secret. When our Shaykh saw him, he extended a rosary to him and said, "Take your rosary." It was in fact his rosary, which he had lost during the invocation.

Sayyidī Shaykh said regarding the Path: "The permission *(idhn)* of our spiritual Path is Mashīshī, which is to say that Shaykh Ibn Mashīsh used to transmit the Light at the moment of initiation as we do today." He also told us about Shaykh Ibn Mashīsh, may God sanctify his secret, "He is known in the assembly of saints *(dīwān al-awliyā')* as the "father of saints" (Abū al-Awliyā')." He says, "I see Shaykh Ibn Mashīsh in flesh and bones, as I see you now. I can even draw each of his features."

One night, when our Shaykh was immersed in the sacred presence, Sayyidī Shaykh Ibn Mashīsh came to visit him and asked him to buy a cloth to cover his shrine *(maqām)*. Sayyidī Shaykh Mohamed Faouzi then saw with the site of the shrine with uncanny precision, along with its layout and the doors leading thereto. Then Sayyidī Ibn Mashīsh asked our Shaykh to give a certain sum of money to four authorized spiritual functionaries *(muqaddams)* who took care of his tomb.

He conveyed to our Shaykh their names as well as the sum meant for each. Sayyidī Shaykh bought the cloth immediately and gathered the sum meant for the four men. Alas, his disciples' issues and education prevented our Shaykh from going to mount 'Alam where Shaykh Ibn Mashīsh is buried, until he saw

Sayyidī Ibn Mashīsh in a vision during the last third of a night, while his wife had dreamt of a man who had told her, "Why does your husband not come to visit me?" When she started describing him Shaykh Mohamed Faouzi recognized immediately Shaykh Ibn Mashīsh whom he could see in front of him. Thus he decided to go to Mount 'Alam near Tétouan.

He departed with some of his disciples, and when they reached the mountain top where the tomb of Shaykh Ibn Mashīsh is located he went to see the spiritual functionary *(muqqadam)* and told him, "Your name is so and so, and you have three colleagues whose names are so and so." The functionary *(muqqadam)* was surprised and asked our Shaykh who he was. He replied, "Here is a sum of money which you must share with your colleagues. It is not from me but from the one who is buried here."

The man, who was of those gifted with spiritual taste, understood that he was dealing with a knower of God and asked what could he do for our Shaykh. Sayyidī Shaykh told him, "Shaykh Ibn Mashīsh asked me to put this cloth over his tomb, can you help me do it?"

"I will gladly help you," said the man, "but a tree has grown from the tomb, and therefore it is not possible to place a cloth over his tomb."

Sayyidī Shaykh told him, "My vision was clear, and my visions need no metaphorical interpretation *(ta'wīl)*. This is what I saw." He started describing with precision the place of the shrine, its layout, the color of the walls, the doors, and everything contained therein. The functionary *(muqqadam)* recognized the place and cried, "It is the birthplace of Shaykh Ibn Mashīsh! Follow me, I will take you there." When they reached the place, Sayyidī Shaykh recognized the elements from his vision, and placed the cloth he had carried on the station.[38]

I witnessed another of his saintly miracles one day when I was standing with him in the space behind the *zāwiya*, which was surrounded with pigeons. He told me, "Observe this pigeon, it is invoking of the name the All-Merciful *(al-Raḥmān)*, while the other one is invoking the name Allāh." That is how I understood

38 One of the witnesses to this story is Sīdī Said Menouach, also known as *muqqadam* Said.

that he possesses the language of animals,[39] and this is a knowledge that a Karkarī disciple can acquire.

Among his saintly miracles is the descending upon the heart of a disciple of sciences and realizations hitherto unknown to him. Also, he understands the unveilings of his disciples, "Know that before a vision reaches you it passes through the heart of your Shaykh first." Thus, in February 2016 I heard the Shaykh say, "Next month I will bring down visions through the reading of *Lām* of Contraction *(lām al-qabḍ)*." I had decided to verify if this was going to happen as he had indicated it would. During March 2016, exactly one month later, Sīdī Suhayl (also known by the surname Adrien) related his visions to the gathering of the disciples during the Friday *dhikr* session, and all

39 He said, "In the beginning I heard a deafening sound similar to a constant wind, then the sound started diminishing and I was able to hear voices *(hawātif)*." He added, "The disciple who penetrates this science must first understand its outward elements before considering the sounds coming from his own body, otherwise he risks losing his mind." He who succeeds in understanding the language of the angels comprehends things distant and near. He perceives the glorification *(tasbīḥ)* of the mineral kingdom, the animal kingdom, and the microcosm. He understands languages which were hitherto completely foreign, as well as other things.

these visions concerned the second reading, namely that of the *Lām* of Contraction.

Another of his saintly miracles is that all his supplications are answered. A great number of persons who suffered from an illness or sought relief from their troubles were cured through the intermediary of the supplications of this noble Shaykh. As an example, I can mention the following anecdote related by Sayyidī Abdel-Nasser:

"In the beginning of the Path I was a young, penniless man. I asked Sayyidī Shaykh several times to supplicate to God to ease my financial situation so that I could help the Path and satisfy my family, but he declined. One Friday while we were at the mosque I seized my opportunity. This time he was staring at the ground, and he started repeating the following words several times, 'May God grant you the herebelow *(dunyā)*![40] May God grant you the herebelow! May God grant you the herebelow!' Ever since that day my situation improved so much that now I find myself immersed in blessings, and I no longer know what

40 The lower world.

to do... I give, I build, I distribute, and the blessings keep coming. Some time ago, I went back to Sayyidī Shaykh in tears to complain from fear that this could distance me from God. He said to me in a smile, 'Be patient.'"

Conclusion

At the end of this booklet which we pray the reader has found beneficial I implore God to cover us with His mercy and to include us with those brought nigh, those who prostrate under the shade of His Throne, on the day when no shade will remain except His shade. May God enable us to follow the footsteps of our Shaykh, to become extinguished in his name and in his form, in order to perfect our characters until we extinguish ourselves in the presence of our Liege-lord and Prophet, *Sayyidunā* Muḥammad ﷺ. May God ennoble us and cover us with His Lights until He is our hearing and our other senses, and until nothing remains but Him.

FSC

Print by
BoD – Books on Demand,
Norderstedt, Germany.

CPSIA information can be obtained
at www.ICGtesting.com
Printed in the USA
LVHW041517311219
642202LV00002B/312

9 782930 978406